WALES
Land of My Fathers

SELECT
EDITIONS

WALES
Land of My Fathers

Alex Hook

SELECT
EDITIONS

Published 2004 in the UK exclusively for

SELECTABOOK
Folly road,
Roundway,
Devises,
Wiltshire
SN10 2HT

All enquiries please email selectabookltd@tiscali.co.uk

All notations of errors or omissions (author inquiries, permissions) concerning the content of this book should be addressed to TAJ Books 27, Ferndown Gardens, Cobham, Surrey, UK, KT11 2BH, info@tajbooks.com.

ISBN 1-84406-033-0

Printed in China.
1 2 3 4 5 08 07 06 05 04

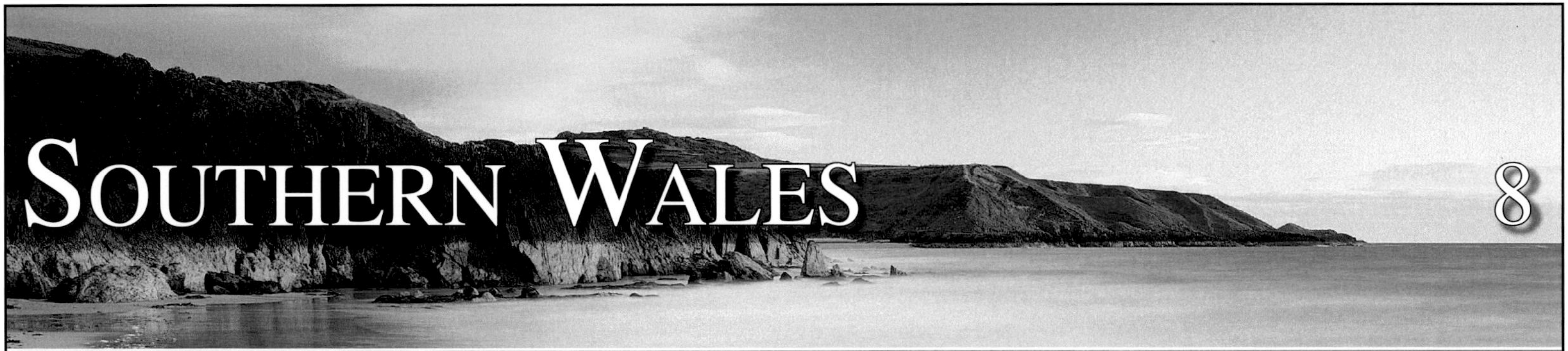

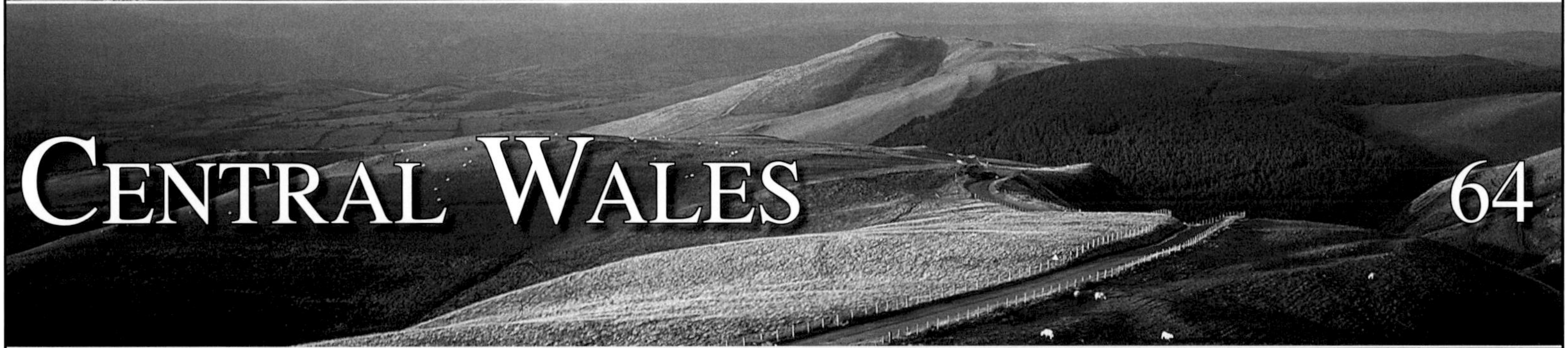

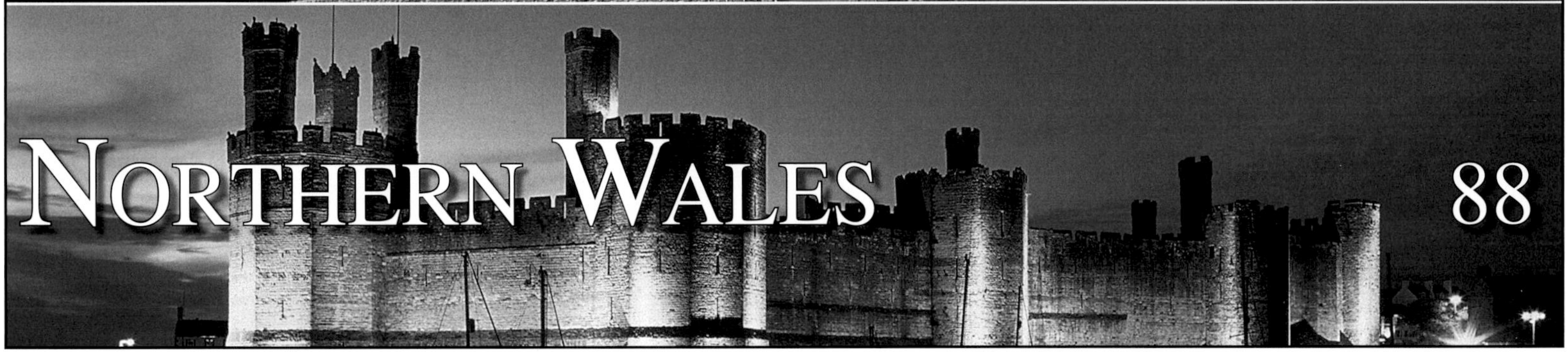

Introduction

Clwyd—Wales—is a land of mountains and valleys, and so much more. It is very different in character between north and south, mountain and coast, town and country. The ancient heritage of Wales is apparent all over the country in the form of its language, buildings, tombs and ancient monuments. Wales is rich in legends and stories that perpetuate the folk laws and traditions of this magical land.

One of the great demarcations between Wales and England is Offa's Dyke. Built by Offa, the King of Mercia in the eighth century, it is a giant earthwork in the form of a bank and ditch running almost complete from Prestatyn on the North Wales coast, to Wye in the south. The dyke marked out the continually disputed border between Celtic Wales and Saxon Mercia. There is now a tough but walkable pathway for 177 miles beside the Dyke, established by the Countryside Commission in 1971.

South Wales is the most populous part of the country; the famous Welsh Valleys are here and it was here that the Industrial Revolution brought prosperity and people looking for work. Just before World War 2 over half the population of Wales lived in Glamorgan. Two important cities sit on the coast, Cardiff at the mouth of the River Severn and Swansea further west on the Bristol Channel. The former is the capital of Wales and sits at the estuaries of the rivers Rhymney, Taff and Ely. There was already a settlement here when the Romans made Cardiff an important town and built a castle, and Cardiff has grown over the centuries into an important political and cultural centre.

Swansea sits at the base of the Gower peninsula and was possibly founded by the Vikings. It became a big industrial city in the 19th century exporting iron, steel and particularly coal. The nearby Gower is an 18 mile long peninsula of limestone headlands and sandy bays; it is an area of outstanding natural beauty.

The once great industrial town of Merthyr Tydfil lies inland in the Taff Valley on the edge of a huge coalfield. In the mid-19th century iron made

Merthyr the largest and most populous town in Wales and it became the largest steel and iron centre of manufacture in the world. But after World War I the heavy industry moved to the coast and the iron works closed in 1930.

West Wales is altogether less developed although its wonderful coastline attracts visitors year-round. The small town of St. David's (after the patron saint of Wales), has a cathedral and was an important centre of Christianity in early times. On the north Pembroke coast is Fishguard, from here boats cross the Irish Sea to Cork and Rosslare.

Mid-Wales is less discovered by visitors but there is plenty to see and do. Towns such as Llandrindod Wells and Builth Wells are ideal locations for exploring the wonderful surrounding countryside. To the south lie the Brecon Beacons National Park and east of them, the Black Mountains. North Wales, too. is mountainous with the massive presence of Snowdonia dominating all.

Caernarfon sits on the Menai Straits opposite the island of Anglesey. It is most famous for its huge fortified castle, built by Edward I of England to establish his hold over the unruly Welsh.

Anglesey's main town is Holyhead. Early Christians settled here in the sixth century, and the church, although built much later, is still very old.

The centre of North Wales is Wrexham , not far from the border with England. Coal, iron and steel formed the backbone of Wrexham during Victorian times but these once huge industries have gone now and the town is much quieter for it. It has a magnificent ornamental church, the Church of St Giles, built in 1472 and considered one of the very finest in Wales.

SOUTHERN WALES

Penarth Marina (left)

Penarth Marina is situated within Cardiff Bay and built around the basins of the historic Penarth Docks.

Severn Road Bridge (above)

The bridge linking England and Wales over the River Severn, or Afon Hafren in Welsh, took five years to build, between 1992 and 1996. The total length is just over 16,404ft.

Nash Point (right)

The stratified cliffs of Nash Point are a designated heritage coast. The cliffs have been eroded by the waves to form a strange-looking series of steps.

Southerndown Beach
(above)
Located on the Glamorgan Heritage Coast, this sandy
expanse backed by dramatic cliffs is one of the most
popular locations to visit in the region. The area has the
second largest tidal range in the world.

Offa's Dyke
(right)
Running for 177 miles from Sedbury Cliffs on the Severn
Estuary near Chepstow to the North Wales resort of
Prestatyn on Liverpool Bay, the Offa's Dyke Path follows
the course of the 8th century Offa's Dyke earthwork for
much of the way.

Cardiff City Hall (left and right)

A 194ft clock tower and dome topped by a fierce Welsh dragon are among the hallmarks of Cardiff City Hall. Built of white Portland stone, City Hall is one of the landmarks of Cardiff city centre and forms the focal point of the civic centre buildings. Inside is the Marble Hall which has a series of statues of Welsh heroes, including St. David, patron saint of Wales, Owen Glyndwr, and Harri Tewdwr, who as Henry VII founded the Tudor dynasty. Taking its name from Roman general Aulus Didius—Caer Didi means Fort of Didius, Cardiff has a long history. At its commercial peak in 1913 Cardiff was biggest coal-exporting port in the world. In 1955 it was proclaimed capital of Wales.

**Museum of Welsh Life
(above and left)**
Located at St. Fagans just outside Cardiff every hour during the day, the museum provides a glimpse of Welsh life in centuries past. There is a superb collection of more than 30 traditional buildings distributed over 100 acres of parkland. Also on the grounds is St. Fagan's Castle, a 16th-century mansion.

**Techniquest, Cardiff
(right)**
This is a hands-on science discovery centre with 160 interactive exhibits, a planetarium, a laboratory, a discovery room, and a hi-tech science theatre.

Cardiff Castle
(left)
Maintained by the council since 1947, the castle dates
back to Norman times although the exterior was greatly
redesigned to fit the fantasies of the 3rd Marquess of
Bute—epitomised by the remarkable Clock Tower.

Cardiff Millennium Stadium
(right)
Fifty-six thousand tonnes of concrete and steel created
the new Millennium Stadium which rose like a phoenix
from the debris of the old Arms Park rugby ground. Quite
simply, it is the best sports arena in Great Britain.

Newport Steel Wave (left)

One of the most striking features of Newport is Peter Fink's extraordinary Steel Wave. Erected in 1990, it was built in recognition of Newport's debt to its steel industry.

Cardiff Bay (above)

The red-brick Pierhead building holds the offices of Associated British Ports in Cardiff. The more modern Atradius building, houses the commercial undertaking that took over the Government's Export Credits Guarantee Department (ECGD) when it was privatised.

The National Museum and Art Gallery of Wales (right)

Situated in the civic centre next to Cardiff City Hall, the museum contains many art treasures and interesting exhibits and is open daily.

Chepstow Castle (left)
A Norman castle high above the river Wye in southeast Wales, building began in 1067, less than a year after William the Conqueror was crowned King of England.

Newcastle Castle, Bridgend (above)
Built in the late 1180s over an earlier building by Henry II, the most outstanding feature of the castle is the Romanesque doorway.

Newport Transporter Bridge (right)
Crossing the River Usk where the land on both sides is low, the 225ft-high bridge consists of a high suspension span supporting a movable carriage which can ferry up to six cars at any one time, as well as pedestrians and cyclists.

Duffryn Gardens (left)
These Grade I-listed Edwardian gardens are in the process of being restored to the original design drawn up by Thomas Mawson in 1904.

National Botanic Garden (above)
The National Botanic Garden of Wales in Carmarthenshire is dedicated to science, education, and leisure alongside the broad study of plants and the environment.

The Mumbles (right)
The lighthouse on the outer island off Mumbles Head was built in 1794 to warn shipping of the dangerous Mixon Sands and Cherry Stone rock. The town of Oystermouth is in the foreground.

Three Cliffs Bay (left)

One of the most photographed places on the Gower Peninsula, the cliffs are popular with climbers and are composed of three linked and pointed faces, their limestone strata punctured by a single-tunnelled archway that leads to Pobbles Beach.

Swansea Marina (above)

Swansea—Abertawe in Welsh—is the gateway to the spectacular Gower peninsula and the second largest town in Wales.

Worms Head (right)

The "Worm" is situated at the southern end of Rhosili Bay, west of Swansea, and is only accessible two and a half hours either side of low water.

Abergavenny (left)

The gateway to the Black Mountains and Brecon Beacons, Abergavenny in the Usk Valley has been an important strategic location since Roman times.

Llandovery (above)

Two famous sons of Llandovery were notorious highwayman Twm Sion Cati (Thomas Jones, 1530–1609) and William Williams, Pantycelyn (1717–91) the Welsh hymn-writer who wrote the words translated as "Guide me o thou great redeemer".

Llyn-y-Fan Fach (right)

This lake is the setting for a famous folktale. A farmer falls in love with a woman who lives in the lake. She agrees to marry him but warns she will leave if he inflicts "three causeless blows". They live happily but three times he strikes her accidentally, and on the third occasion she returns to the lake, taking her cattle with her.

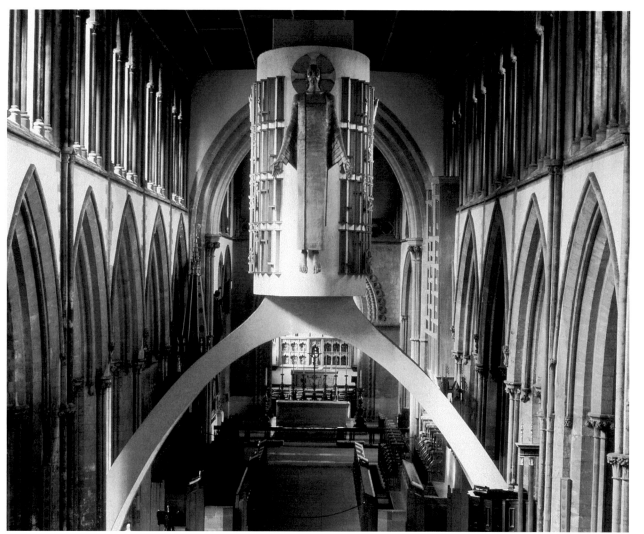

Llandaff Cathedral (left)
One of the oldest Christian sites in Britain, in the 6th century St Dyfrig founded a community close to the ford where the Roman road crossed the River Taff. The present cathedral dates from c.1107-33 but it was not completed enough to dedicate until 1266.

Caerphilly Castle (right)
The first castle in Britain to be built to a concentric design with successive lines of defence set one inside the other, building started in 1268. Cromwell's troops tried to dismantle it, luckily unsuccessfully.

**Bryngarw Country Park
(above)**
Built by John Popkin Traherne in 1834, Bryngarw
House—described as a "small but elegant dwelling"—sits
in 113 acres of Country Parkland.

**Llanthony Priory
(right)**
One of the earliest houses of Augustinian canons to
be founded in Britain, Llanthony Priory sits in the
remote Vale of Ewyas in the Black Mountains. After the
Dissolution the site was sold for about £160, and was left
to decay.

**Parc Howard Museum
(above)**
Housing a renowned collection of Llanelli Pottery and
material related to the history of the town, Parc Howard
was built by the Buckley family in 1885. The house and its
27-acre park, was given to the town of Llanelli in 1912.

**Caldicot Castle
(right)**
Founded by the Normans, developed in royal hands as a
stronghold in the Middle Ages and restored as a Victorian
family home, Caldicot Castle is set in 55 acres of parkland
on the River Neddern.

**Margam Park
(left)**
This fantastic Gothic
mansion house boasts
a magnificent orangery
and is set in 850 acres of
glorious parkland.

**Carreg Cennen Castle
(right)**
Southeast of Llandelio
in South Wales, Carreg
Cennen's history goes
back to neolithic times.
The Romans occupied the
site, too, as did the Welsh
Princes of Deheubarth,
who built the first castle.
The ruins date from a
later period—that of King
Edward I (1272–1307).

Rhondda Heritage Park (left and right)
Based in the stores building of the old Lewis Merthyr colliery, the Rhondda Heritage Park Visitor Centre opened to the public in July 1989. It tells the story of coal—so vital to Wales and Britain—and in July 1994 "A Shift in Time" opened: it includes a cage ride to Pit Bottom, guided tour through the underground roadways of the Lewis Merthyr colliery pre-mechanisation and the working coalface.

Pembrokeshire Coastal path (left)

The 179-mile coast path follows the shoreline of southwestern Wales, starting in the north at St. Dogmaels and passes Fishguard, St. David's, Pembroke and Tenby, ending at Amroth.

Taf Fechan (above)

The Taf Fechan rises in the Brecon Beacons and is a major tributary to the River Taff.

Rhossili (right)

Famous for its spectacular beaches, Rhossili was also appreciated by prehistoric man. Two-chambered tombs of rock were made on the landward slope of Rhossili Down by Stone Age men 6,000 years ago.

The Valleys
(left)
Wales is famous for its spectacular coastline, rugged mountain scenery and lush green valleys.

Caswell
(above)
A sandy beach situated ten minutes' drive from Mumbles village, Caswell is close to the Bishop's Wood nature reserve. There is a coastal path east to Langland Bay with spectacular views across the Bristol Channel to North Devon.

Plinlimon
(right)
In Welsh the mountain is Plumlumon Fawr, 2,468ft on the Powys-Ceredigion border west of Llanidloes. It has three summits and is the source of the Wye, Severn, and other waters.

Monnow Bridge, Monmouth
(left)
Monnow Bridge is the only medieval fortified river bridge in Britain where the gate tower stands on the bridge. The bridge was built in the late 1200s, Monnow Gate at the beginning of the 14th century.

Wye Valley from Wyndcliff
(right)
Wye Valley and Vale of Usk is a land of magnificent scenery and the time-ravaged castles of the Welsh borderlands.

Usk
(left)
The town of Usk nestles alongside the river Usk, its ruined castle dating back to Norman times. In the middle of the town is Twyn Square, with a Victorian clock as its centre piece.

Crickhowell
(above)
A market town situated between the Black Mountains and the Brecon Beacons, Crickhowell is a thriving market town in arguably the most beautiful valley in the National Park.

Brecon Castle
(right)
The castle was built by Bernard de Neufmarche, one of the second generation of conquerors who extended Norman influence into the Marches of Wales. By 1093 he had began to build castles to control their new lands.

Three views of the Brecon Beacons

The Brecon Beacons National Park contains some of the most spectacular and distinctive upland formations in southern Britain. Situated amongst hills and mountains, the Park covers an area of 520 sq miles. Stretching from Hay on Wye in the east to Llandeilo in the west, it incorporates the Black Mountains, the Central Beacons and Fforest Fawr and is looked after by the National Park Authority.

Carew Cross (left)
The cross is 14ft high and carved with intricate Celtic knots and ornaments and dates from the ninth century. It bears the Latin inscription Margiteut Recett Rex, celebrating an early Welsh king.

Aberglasney (above)
Spectacularly set in the beautiful Tywi valley of armarthenshire, Aberglasney Gardens have been an inspiration for poetry and gardeners since 1477.

St. David's Cathedral (right)
Built upon the site of St. David's 6th century monastery, St. David's Cathedral has been a site of pilgrimage and worship for many hundreds of years and remains a church serving a living community.

Carew Castle
(left)
Described by many as the "most handsome in all South Wales", Carew Castle is also the site of the ancient Carew Cross.

Carmarthen
(above)
The castle is the focal point of Carmarthen, the county town of the old Carmarthenshire. Merlin is said to have lived nearby—Carmarthen became in Welsh Caerfyrddin, Merlin's City.

Fishguard
(right)
Fishguard and neighbouring Goodwick are said to have derived their names from the Vikings, who were frequent visitors to this part of the coast.

Strumble Head (left)

The Pembrokeshire Coast Path runs all round this beautiful headland. The entire area is ideal for bird spotting—especially buzzards, peregrines, choughs, and a wide variety of sea birds.

Stack Rocks (above)

Stack Rocks (in Welsh Elegug (guillemot) Stacks are two detached pillars of limestone whose tops and the ledges below are crammed with guillemots and razor-bills.

Burry Port (right)

A small picturesque town situated on the south-west coast of Wales, Burry Port is probably best known for being the arrival point on June 18, 1928, of Amelia Earhart—the first woman to fly solo across the Atlantic.

Whitesands Bay
(above)
One of the most popular beaches in all of Pembrokeshire, Whitesands is a large sandy beach surrounded by magnificent coastline, with views of Ramsey Island and several smaller islets out to sea.

Barafundle Bay
(right)
East-facing, so well sheltered from prevailing winds, Barafundle Bay is owned and managed by the National Trust.

Manorbier (left)

Five miles southwest of Tenby near the Pembrokshire Coast Path, Manorbier boasts an impressive Norman castle and Church of St James.

Dinefwr Park (above)

At the heart of Welsh history for a thousand years, Dinefwr Park took shape in the years after 1775, when the medieval castle, house, gardens, woods and deer park were integrated into one vast and breathtaking landscape

Tenby Harbour (right)

Tenby is both a mediaeval walled town and one of Wales' favourite seaside resorts. Its ancient harbour, surrounded by Regency houses in pastel colours, is a focus for artists and photographers.

Preseli mountain (left)

Legend was that bluestones from the Preseli Mountains were used in the construction of Stonehenge in Wiltshire—some 140 miles by sea and land. Amazingly, this fact was confirmed in modern times.

Bosherston Lakes (above)

Created in the late 18th century by damming three narrow valleys, the lakes are now the centrepiece of an important National Nature Reserve.

Teifi Valley (right)

The River Teifi (TAY-VEE) is one of the longest rivers in Wales joining the three counties of Pembrokeshire, Ceredigion and Carmarthenshire.

Skomer Island (left)

The island is a haven for wildlife and half a million seabirds—fulmars, guillemots, razorbills, kittiwakes, gulls, oystercatchers, curlew and short-eared owls—breed here annually.

Saundersfoot (right)

Saundersfoot Bay Leisure Park is situated in a superb location in one of Wales' most beautiful settings, the Pembrokeshire Coastal National Park.

CENTRAL WALES

Aberdovey
(left)
A thriving little harbour resort set within the Snowdonia National Park, Aberdovey (Aber = river mouth in Welsh) is where the River Dovey meets the blue waters of Cardigan Bay.

Aberaeron
(above)
A charming planned Georgian town located on Cardigan Bay. The well-preserved Georgian facades are mainly painted with architectural details in a contrasting shade.

Machynlleth
(right)
Machynlleth has a special role in Welsh history because of its connection with Owain Glyndwr, who was crowned Prince of Wales in 1404 near the Parliament House.

**Mynach Falls
(left)**
Situated high in the foothills of the Plinlimon mountain range 12 miles east of Aberystwyth, above the Mynach Falls is Devil's Bridge, the original of which dates back to the 11th century.

**Dolgellau
(above and right)**
A small market town situated at the foot of the Cader Idris mountain range in south Snowdonia, Owain Glyndwr held the last Welsh parliament in Dolgellau in 1404. The focal point for the development of the Quakers in the 17th century, this community was one of the main forces for its new homeland in Pennsylvania. "Bryn Mawr" is the name of a local farm in the area which gave its name to the famous university in Pennsylvania.

Aberystwyth (left)

A small seaside town in the county of Ceredigion on the west coast of Wales, Aberystwyth is situated towards the centre of the crescent of Cardigan Bay, its harbour fed by the confluence of the rivers Ystwyth and Rheidol.

Cwmtudu (above)

The little hamlet of Cwmtudu has a smuggling past. The cove and surrounding dark caves were ideal for ships to arrive at the dead of night with their cargoes of salt and brandy.

Harlech (right)

Spectacularly sited, Harlech Castle seems to grow naturally from the rock on which it is perched. Like an all-seeing sentinel, it gazes out across land and sea, keeping a watchful eye over Snowdonia.

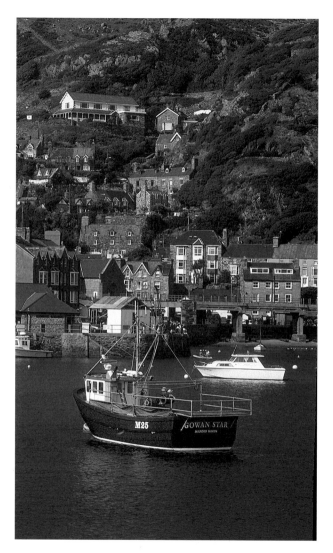

**Barmouth
(left)**
Located on the west coast
of North Wales and lying
between a mountain range
and the sea on the mouth
of the River Mawddach,
Barmouth rests just within
the south-west corner of
Snowdonia National Park.

**Ynys Lochtyn
(above)**
At Llangrannog a
spectacular walk along the
cliffs leads to the National
Trust promontory at Ynys
Lochtyn, near the Iron
Age fortified settlement
Pendinas Lochtyn.

**Mwnt
(right)**
The beautiful beach of
Mwnt has the finest views
over Cardigan Bay.

Caban Coch Reservoir (left)

The lowest of the dams in the sequence of four built in the valley of the Elan River is Caban Coch dam. The lake formed is nearly 500 acres in size.

Llandrindod Wells (above)

The county town of Powys since 1974, prior to that Llandrindod Wells was the administrative centre for the County of Radnor.

New Quay (right)

Ceinewydd in Welsh, New Quay climbs a hill overlooking Cardigan Bay: Bottlenose dolphins can be observed from the shore.

**Lake Vyrnwy
(left)**
Man-made, with the dam
that created it completed
in 1888, the village of
Llanwddyn was submerged
by Lake Vyrnwy, which is
one of the biggest man-
made lakes in Wales.

**Llyn Brianne Reservoir
(above and right)**
Situated on the headwaters of the river Towy, near its
source in the Cambrian Mountains, the reservoir is meant
to supplement the main river during low flows. Beautiful,
romantic and still quite unspoilt, the Towy rises some way
up the valley past Nantystalwyn,

Mawddach River (left)

This nature reserve is situated in the superb scenery of the Mawddach Valley and offers beautiful walks through oak woodland.

Llynnau Cregennen (above)

The Llynnau Cregennen are two tarns high up—some 800ft behind Arthog—on the western slopes of the Cader Idris range, overlooking the Mawddach estuary.

Craig Goch (right)

The dam at Craig Goch, the highest upstream of the series of dams in the Elan Valley, is often referred to as the top dam. It is located at a height of 1,040 feet (317m) above sea level.

Cardigan Bay (left)

Yachting and sailing in Cardigan Bay is a particular enjoyment for this who wish to see dolphins.

Berriew (above)

Berriew means the place where the Rhiw flows into the River Severn. At the confluence is a village in the heart of the Welsh border country, a few miles southwest of Welshpool.

River Banwy (right)

Rural in character, the thinly populated central region is the most peaceful and least explored part of Wales. This is the River Banwy, a tributary of the River Vyrnwy, bridged by the Welshpool & Llanfair Light Railway.

Llanddewi Brefi (left)

A pretty rural village, Llanddewi Brefi is noted for its handsome church on the site of which St David is reputed to have performed a miracle.

Strata Florida (above)

The name is a Latinised from of the Welsh Ystrad Fflur—wide valley or plain of flowers. The abbey was founded by the Cistercians in 1164 and was dissolved by Henry VIII in 1539.

Mountain Biking (right)

The beautiful browns of the mountains contrasts vividly with the lush green valleys.

Criccieth Castle (left)

Standing on headland between two beaches overlooking Tremadog Bay, the core of the castle was built by Llywelyn the Great; it was taken by Edward I's forces in 1283 and extensively refortified.

Llanidloes (above)

Wales's only remaining Market Hall (built in 1609) stands at the centre of Llanidloes. The town's most significant moment came in 1839 when it became a hotbed of Chartists.

Llangrannog (right)

Llangrannog has a special significance within Wales for nearby is a residential facility operated by Urdd Gobaith Cymru—Wales's League of Youth. Generation after generation of Welsh children have spent a holiday here.

**Portmeirion
(left and right)**
An Italianate village, famous as the setting for "The Prisoner", Portmeirion was designed by Clough Williams-Ellis. It has other film involvement—Noel Coward's Blythe Spirit was written there.

NORTHERN WALES

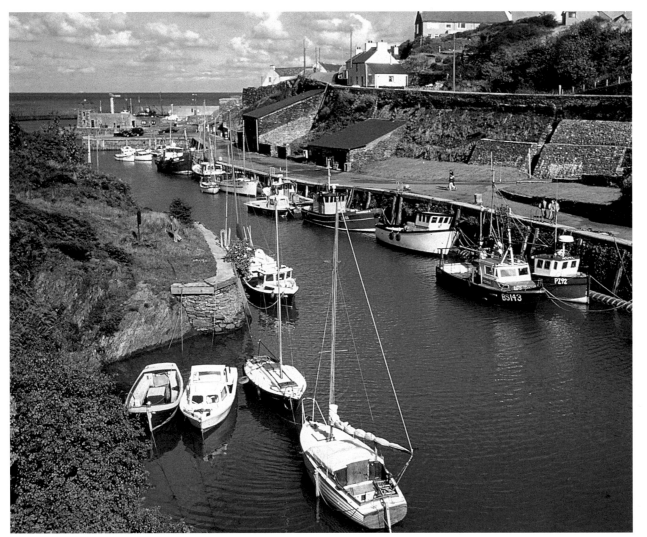

Amlwch
(left)
Situated on the northeastern corner of Anglesey, Amlwch is a small town with a long history dating back to the Bronze Age when it was an important location for trading the copper from Anglesey's Parys Mountain mines.

Trearddur Bay
(right)
One of Wales' best beaches and most romantic locations, Trearddur Bay on Anglesey is just minutes from Holyhead on Holy Island.

**Llanfair Pg
(left)**
Its full name is
"Llanfairpwllgwyngyll goge
rychwyrndrobwllllantysilio
gogogoch". It was reputedly
invented by an innkeeper
during the last century to
drum up more trade from
train travellers.

**Menai Bridge
(right)**
The total length of the
bridge is 1,500ft; part of
which is supported by the
three arched piers on the
mainland side and four
piers on the Anglesey
side. The suspended
span between the two
"pyramids" is 580ft.

Bardsley Island (left)

For many centuries, Bardsley Island, two miles off the mainland of Caernarvonshire, was an important place of pilgrimage—tradition asserts that 20,000 monks are buried there.

Beaumaris (above and right)

King Edward I built a magnificent castle at Beaumaris on the Menai Straits. Begun in 1295, it was the last of the great castles Edward put in place to subjugate the Welsh. The town is interesting, too: explore the atmospheric interiors of the Victorian gaol and courthouse.

Penrhyn Castle (left)

Situated between Snowdonia and the Menai Strait, Penrhyn Castle is a fine piece of neo-Norman architecture, built between 1827 and 1846.

Llanbedrog (above)

One of the key centres of the Lleyn Peninsula, the village gets its name because of the establishment of the church, which is attributed to St Pedrog who lived in the 6th century.

Llandudno (right)

The largest resort in Wales, Llandudno is situated between the Great and Little Ormes with two wonderful beaches, the award-winning North Shore and the quiet, sand-duned West Shore.

Llanberis Lake Railway (left)

Starting at Gilfach Ddu station in the Padarn Park at Llanberis, the trains take approximately 40 minutes to make the journey to Penllyn and back.

Abersoch (above)

Situated on the Lleyn Peninsula, Abersoch has become a very popular village seaside resort known foremost for sailing and fishing.

Aberglaslyn Pass (right)

Known for its impressive waterfalls, Sygun Copper Mine and the spectacular scenery of the unspoilt Lleyn Peninsula, the Aberglaslyn Pass allows the River Glaslyn to cut its way out of Snowdonia to the sea.

Llanddwyn Island (left)

It is not quite an island: it remains attached to the mainland at all but the highest tides. It provides excellent views of Snowdonia and the Lleyn Peninsula and is part of the Newborough Warren National Nature Reserve.

Llanddwyn Island (left)

It is not quite an island: it remains attached to the mainland at all but the highest tides. It provides excellent views of Snowdonia and the Lleyn Peninsula and is part of the Newborough Warren National Nature Reserve.

Aberdaron (right)

An old whitewashed fishing village situated at the western tip of North Wales, Aberdaron church is extraordinarily old, dating back to the Celtic era before the mission of St Augustine in the late 7th century.

Pwllheli
(left)
Situated on the south side of the Lleyn and is the capital of the peninsula, Pwllheli provides access to some of the best sailing waters in the UK including Cardigan Bay, Anglesey and the attractive harbours along Ireland's east coast.

Porth Dinllaen
(above)
On the north-facing coast of the Lleyn Peninsula, the remote 18th-century fishing village of Porth Dinllaen nestles on the edge of a beautiful beach.

Beddgelert
(right)
Named after Gelert, the faithful hound of Prince Llywelyn the Great. Llywelyn returned home to find his hound, whom he had left to protect his son, covered with blood. Fearing the worst he killed it—only to discover that the blood was from a wolf Gelert had killed in defence of his heir.

Betws-y-Coed (left)
The principal village of the Snowdonia National Park, Betws-y-Coed is the perfect centre from which to explore the jewel of North Wales: Snowdon itself.

South Stack (above)
Over 4,000 pairs of seabirds breed on the cliffs at South Stack, on the Isle of Anglesey, every year. Between April and July you can watch them from the Ellin's Tower centre.

Conwy (right)
A classic walled town, Conwy's circuit of walls, over three-quarters of a mile long and guarded by no fewer than 22 towers, is one of the finest in the world.

Conwy Valley (left)
The valley proper begins at the Conwy Falls situated above the confluence with the River Lledr close to Betws-y-Coed, the starting point for many forest and lake walks.

Llanrwst (above)
Situated in the Conwy Valley to the north of Betws-y-Coed, Llanrwst is a busy market town.

Bodnant Garden (right)
One of Britain's most spectacular gardens, situated above the River Conwy with stunning views across Snowdonia, Bodnant was laid out in 1847 and given to the National Trust in 1949 by Lord Aberconway.

Caernarfon
(left)
Lying on the Menai Straits where the River Seiont reaches
the sea, Caernarfon was settled by the Celts before the
Romans came or before Edward I built his great castle
there.

Dolbadarn Castle
(right)
Dolbadarn Castle stands above Llyn Padarn, between
Caernarfon and Snowdonia. Built by the Welsh Princes it
dates to the 13th century.

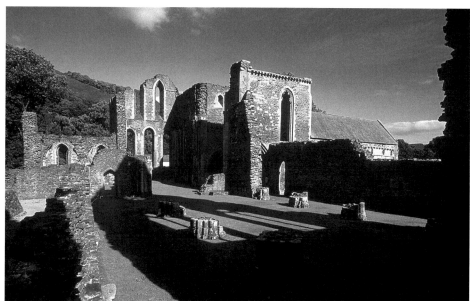

Ceiriog Valley (left)
A place of mountains and valleys, rivers and waterfalls, it is bounded by the rugged grandeur of the Berwyn Mountains, rising at Cader Fronwen to some 2,300ft and by the tributaries of the Vyrnwy and Severn rivers.

Valle Crucis Abbey (above)
Near Llangollen, Valle Crucis was founded in 1189 and dissolved by Henry VIII. What's left shows off the Early English style of architecture.

Conwy Castle (right)
By any standards one of the great fortresses of medieval Europe, it was built by Edward I. Conwy today is also known for Telford's suspension bridge built across the estuary in 1827.

Tal-y-Cafn
(left)
At Tal-y-Cafn the Conwy valley line from Llandudno Junction passes close to the site of a Roman encampment, Caerhun. The bridge at Tal-y-Cafn is the first crossing place of the river from Conwy. It was built in 1897 to replace the ferry.

Colwyn Bay
(above)
Designed by Maynall and Littlewood of Manchester, Colwyn Bay Victoria Pier was one of the later British piers to be built, opening on June 1, 1900.

Gwynant
(right)
Beneath Snowdon is Nant Gwynant, one of Wales's most lovely valleys. It lies between Beddgelert and Penygwryd and within it are two lakes—Llyn Dinas, named after the lakeside iron-age hill fort of Dinas Emrys, and Llyn Gwynant.

Snowdonia

Snowdon dominates the ancient landscape of North Wales. At 3,560ft (1085m) it is a true mountain and a place of legend - said to be the burial place of the giant ogre Rhita, vanquished by King Arthur. Since 1896, the Snowdon Mountain Railway has made it easy to get to the top under someone else's steam. Uniquely in Britain, it is a rack and pinion railway that runs from Llanberis to within 66ft of the summit of the highest mountain in England and Wales.

Snowdonia

Snowdonia National Park is in the county of Gwynedd and is very popular with tourists, especially for hiking. Snowdon is understandably the greatest attraction. There are several paths up Snowdon of different lengths and difficulties, ranging from the very easy (but long) Llanberis path to the knife-edge Crib Goch ridge.

Rhyl
(left)
Six miles of golden sands stretch between the resorts of Rhyl and Prestatyn The beach at Rhyl is north facing. The tidal range is large, exposing many sandbanks. At the western boundary are the Clwyd Estuary and Rhyl Harbour.

Horseshoe Pass
(above)
The Horseshoe Pass near Llangollen. At the top is the Ponderosa cafe—well known to motorcyclists—from where many scenic routes start.

Talyllyn Railway
(right)
An historic narrow-gauge steam railway running from Tywyn to Abergynolwyn and Nant Gwernol, the line passes the delightful Dolgoch Falls

Moelfre (left)

Moelfre (y Moel + fre—the bare hill) looks like every child's idea of a seaside village—picturesque port, beach, fine views of Snowdonia, and a working lifeboat.

Mold (above)

There is known to have been a settlement at or near Mold since the Bronze Age. The famous Welsh novelist Daniel Owen was born here and there is a community centre named after him in the town.

Llangollen (right)

Llangollen nestles within the beautiful Dee Valley in northeast Wales. It is host to the International Musical Eisteddfod.

Llechwedd (left)

Llechwedd Slate Caverns offer a choice of two spectacular rides into the vast slate mines of Blaenau Ffestiniog.

Pistyll Rhaeadr (above)

Translated as the "spring of the waterfall", the impressive cascade is the highest in Wales at 240ft. It is difficult to get to and is best visited from Llanfyllin.

Moel Famau Country Park (right)

With 2,000 acres of impressive, colourful heather moorland, a haven for wildlife like birds of prey, Moel Famau Country Park forms part of the Clwydian Range Area of Outstanding Natural Beauty.

Ruthin
(left)
Built on a red sandstone hill as a strategic lookout over the River Clwyd, Ruthin has over 700 years of recorded history.

Swallow Falls
(above)
In Welsh Rhaeadr Ewynnol, this waterfall on the River Llugwy has become a familiar celebrity on film, postcard and canvas.

Yr Eifl
(right)
Above Llanaelhaern is one of Britain's most spectacular hillforts—Tre'r Ceiri, meaning "Town of the Giants".

Outdoor holidays

Wales is a wonderful place for outdoor holidays. These photographs show Criccieth on the Llyn Peninsula (left), the Nefyn and District Golf Club at Morfa Nefyn, Gwynedd, North Wales, and the impressive Cader Idris, South Snowdonia. But Wales is also a land of legends: locals claim that the mountain is haunted, and that anyone who spends the night on top of Cader Idris will wake up either a madman or a poet.